Dump Trucks

Blaine Wiseman

WEIGL PUBLISHERS INC.
"Creating Inspired Learning"
www.weigl.com

Published by Weigl Publishers Inc.
350 5th Avenue, 59th Floor
New York, NY 10118
Website: www.weigl.com

Library of Congress Cataloging-in-Publication Data available upon request.
Fax 1-866-44-WEIGL for the attention of the Publishing Records department.

ISBN 978-1-61690-145-5 (hard cover)
ISBN 978-1-61690-146-2 (soft cover)

Printed in the United States of America in North Mankato, Minnesota
1 2 3 4 5 6 7 8 9 0 14 13 12 11 10

052010
WEP264000

Editor: Heather C. Hudak
Design: Terry Paulhus

All of the Internet URLs given in the book were valid at the time of publication. However, due to the dynamic nature of the Internet, some addresses may have changed, or sites may have ceased to exist since publication. While the author and publisher regret any inconvenience this may cause readers, no responsibility for any such changes can be accepted by either the author or the publisher.

Every reasonable effort has been made to trace ownership and to obtain permission to reprint copyright material. The publishers would be pleased to have any errors or omissions brought to their attention so that they may be corrected in subsequent printings.

Weigl acknowledges Getty Images as its primary image supplier for this title.

CONTENTS

4 What are Dump Trucks?

7 Tremendous Trucks

8 Teamwork

10 Heavy Duty

13 Fill It Up

14 Dump It Out

16 Truck Travels

18 License to Drive

20 Backing Up

22 Build Your Own Dump Truck

23 Find Out More

24 Glossary/Index

What are Dump Trucks?

How do workers move dirt, rocks, and other objects around a work site? They use big machines called dump trucks. These huge trucks have a big box on the back that can be filled with objects. The truck moves to a new place and dumps the objects out.

In England and Australia, dump trucks are called "tippers." This is because the box tips backward when it dumps a load.

Tremendous Trucks

Did you know that the world's biggest dump trucks are so large that they cannot fit on a regular road? The trucks are brought to the work site in pieces and put together there. These trucks are used for mining. They can carry a load weighing about as much as 5,000 people.

Each tire on these trucks is 13 feet (4 meters) tall and weighs 116,800 pounds (52,980 kg). A new tire costs $25,000.

Each tire is held in place by 47 **nuts**. Most car tires are held on by five nuts.

Teamwork

Did you know that dump trucks do not work alone? Other big machines pick up objects and place them in the box of the dump truck. The dump truck then moves the objects to a new place.

Some dump trucks pull separate trailers behind them. These are called transfer dump trucks. Many objects can be carried in the trailer.

Heavy Duty

Why are dump trucks able to carry so much weight? Dump trucks are made from strong, sturdy materials. The truck's tires are made of thick rubber. This allows for huge loads to be placed in the back of a dump truck without putting too much weight on the tires.

Dump trucks have huge engines. These engines have extra power for carrying heavy loads. The solid metal box on the back of the truck keeps the load from falling out.

Fill It Up

Did you know that the biggest dump trucks can hold as much as 1,800 gallons (6,814 liters) of fuel? This is 50 times more than the average pickup truck.

Some dump trucks use **electric** power as well as fuel. They have a **battery** pack that supplies energy to help move the truck.

Dump It Out

How does a dump truck dump its load? The truck driver moves a lever to lift the box and dump the load. Moving the lever pushes oil in the motor from one tube to another. This creates power and makes the box rise.

Some truck drivers can raise the box, dump the load, and lower the box in only 20 seconds.

Truck Travels

How fast can a dump truck travel? Some large dump trucks can reach 40 to 50 miles (64 to 81 kilometers) per hour. Small dump trucks can travel at higher speeds.

Dump trucks can tip over easily. For this reason, drivers often stay below the speed limit on major routes.

License to Drive

Does it take special training to drive a dump truck? Dump trucks are more difficult to drive than smaller vehicles. Drivers must have special licenses to drive these big machines.

Drivers must know how to cover the truck's load with a **tarp**. The tarp will keep objects from flying out of the box. Drivers are taught to lower the box before moving the truck. A raised box can get caught on wires or signs.

Backing Up

Have you ever used a mirror to look at the back of your head? Dump truck drivers use mirrors in much the same way. Mirrors on the side of the truck help the driver see the area behind the truck. However, there are still places the driver cannot see. Spotters are people who stand behind the truck and tell the driver if there are objects in the truck's path.

Some spotters use flags or radios to signal the driver. Most use hand signals. The spotter points in a certain direction to show the driver which way to turn. Spotters slowly bring their hands together to tell the driver when to stop moving.

21

Build Your Own Dump Truck

eight-cup egg carton   scissors   glue   markers

1. With an adult's help, cut off the top of the egg carton. Then, cut off about one-third of the top part. This will be the truck box.

2. Next, cut off the first two egg cups from the bottom of the carton. You should have two pieces, one with two cups and another with six cups. The two cups will be the cab of the truck. The six cups will be the base.

3. Cut off the bottom of the two cups in the center of the six-cup base. Then, turn the base so that the four remaining cups are sitting on the work surface.

4. Glue the two-cup piece on top of the front of the six-cup piece. Make sure the egg cups are facing upward.

5. Now, glue the box of the truck on the back of the base.

6. Decorate the truck using the markers. Make sure to draw windows, doors, and tires.

Find Out More

To learn more about dump trucks, visit these websites.

How Stuff Works
http://auto.howstuffworks.com/biggest-truck-in-the-world.htm

Truck Driving School
www.driving-truck-school.com/dump_truck_driving_tips.html

Everything About Construction
www.kenkenkikki.jp/
special/no08/e_index.html

Glossary

battery: a device that produces electricity

electric: uses, provides, or is powered by electricity

nuts: metal rings used to hold screws in place

tarp: waterproof canvas or plastic sheet that is used to cover objects

Index

box 4, 8, 10, 14, 18, 22

driver 14, 16, 18, 20

electric 13

license 18

power 10, 13, 14

speed 16
spotters 20

tires 7, 10, 22